The Elga'

Birthplace

and Visitor Centre

Contents

THIS WAY TO THE BIRTHPLACE

Published in
Great Britain by

Elgar Editions

for

Elgar Foundation Enterprises Ltd
The Elgar Birthplace Museum, Crown East Lane,
Lower Broadheath, Worcester WR2 6RH

© Elgar Foundation Enterprises Ltd, 2004

First Published : August 2004

British Library Cataloguing in Publication Data
A Catalogue record for this book
is available from the British Library

ISBN 0 9537082 8 4 (Elgar Editions)

Acknowledgements:
The Elgar Will Trust
Chris Bennett
Bill Meadows
Michael Messenger O.B.E.
Andrew Neill
John Norris
Arthur Reynolds
Catherine Sloan
Ann Vernau

Printed and bound in Great Britain by
Pershore Print
49 High Street, Pershore
Worcestershire WR10 1EU

Photo: **Touchstones** at the Elgar Birthplace Museum,
by Claire Whitcomb and students from Worcestershire LEA Schools

Welcome to the Elgar Birthplace, the only museum entirely devoted to the life and work of Sir Edward Elgar, one of only a handful of truly great composers produced by this country. Indeed, many would argue that, having regard to the esteem in which he is held by the musical fraternity coupled with the popular appeal of much of his music, he is Britain's greatest ever composer.

He was born in 1857, here in Broadheath in the small cottage which forms part of the present Museum, and his enduring affection for his birthplace is reflected in his decision to adopt the title of Broadheath when he was awarded a baronetcy in 1931, less than three years before his death. His daughter Carice was adamant that it was his wish that the modest cottage that had seen his birth rather than the many grander houses in which he lived during his long and active life, should be the place where he was commemorated. She it was who persuaded Worcester Corporation to acquire the property in 1935, then leasing it to a trust to operate. She also contacted many friends and acquaintances, gathering letters, scores and other memorabilia to form a worthy and representative collection reflecting her late father's life, interests and, of course, work. Those efforts, coupled with a major national appeal held at the time, resulted in a collection of almost unrivalled richness, and form the core of the present day Museum and Archive.

The Birthplace itself, for many years the only building here, was first opened to the public during the 1930s, initially on an occasional basis, but gradually the frequency was increased until the Museum was open for much of the week during all but the winter months. Carice Elgar Blake died in 1970 but already the collection had outgrown the Birthplace Cottage and the need for additional accommodation was recognised. In the early 1990s a start was made on a new Centre, adjacent to the Birthplace Cottage, but it was several years before it could finally be completed. It was officially opened by Dame Janet Baker on 19 October 2000.

The Centre, with its environmentally controlled cases, provides an opportunity to display rare manuscripts and other original archival material, and through those and a range of modern audio-visual aids, to explore the musical genius and achievements of Elgar. The Cottage retains a much more domestic feel with a far greater concentration upon Elgar the man, beginning with his early life and upbringing. His essentially modest origins are clear and those, coupled with his Roman Catholicism in staunchly Protestant late nineteenth century England, made his subsequent achievements all the more remarkable. He was a complex man with a wide range of interests beyond composing, as the displays clearly demonstrate, and the span of his music is no less extraordinary; there is far more to Elgar than the Pomp and Circumstance of Edwardian England, as the Enigma Variations, the great oratorios, the symphonies, and the chamber music composed in the wake of the devastation of World War I eloquently testify – all are reflected within the Elgar Birthplace and Centre.

We trust that you find your visit both instructive and immensely enjoyable.

Michael Messenger
Chairman,
Elgar Birthplace
Management
Committee,
March, 2004

Personal Memories . . .

When you have seen the little house where my father was born and its collection of intimate personal belongings which he constantly used, you may be interested to read an impression of him, and which may serve to bring to life the picture you may have formed of him from your visit to his birthplace and your knowledge of his music and life.

He was tall, with a slight stoop, and looked more like a military officer than an artist, being often mistaken for the late Duke of Connaught. To describe his personality is almost impossible, for he showed a different side of his many-faceted nature to each person. His human understanding and vast fund of knowledge on nearly every subject made him able to enter into the interests of everyone he met with real sympathy. I think it is generally known that the last subject he could be induced to talk about [except to a chosen few] was music, and people were astonished at his ready response to their interests instead of having, as they naturally expected, to confine their conversation to purely musical subjects.

Though in their early married days my parents had a hard struggle, there was a feeling of enthusiasm and aspiration which never waned as years went by. My father worked hard composing and teaching, and my mother struggled with the household problems protecting him all the time from unnecessary worries; but always there existed friendship, gaiety, liveliness, a sense of humour and, above all, compassion for others.

In the forefront of their lives was the ideal of beauty. My mother shared my father's tastes and was his constant companion in leisure hours, when they enjoyed reading poetry and studying the masterpieces of painting and sculpture; nor must I forget their passionate love of nature and outdoor life. New ideas and inventions were never shut out, but embraced with enthusiasm. In spite of every obstacle, the picture is one of happiness and continual striving for the ideal, my mother self-sacrificingly smoothing away all worries from my father's path and helping him in every way to make the career which she never for a moment doubted was to be his —with what result, we all now know.

Carice Elgar Blake

Edward Elgar was born, the fourth of seven children, on the upper floor of this little cottage on 2 June 1857. He was surely, as one writer has claimed, 'the last of the great British Musicians to spring from the common people.' William Elgar, his father, an itinerant piano tuner, had taken his family into the country out of the city of Worcester the previous year. Their stay in the village of Broadheath was short, Edward being the only child born there, for the family returned to the city in 1859. In due course William Elgar established a music business in Worcester's High Street and it was there that Edward grew up.

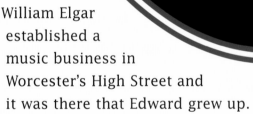

He was to marry in 1889 and did not return to live permanently in Worcester until 1929 where he remained until his death in early 1934. In the intervening years his musical success and growing fame enabled him to live in large homes such as Plas Gwyn in Hereford and Severn House in Hampstead. Marl Bank on Worcester's Rainbow Hill, his last home, was an imposing building too, with a fine view of the Cathedral. However, it was this small cottage which Elgar chose as his memorial.

Despite his awards and fame as well as his position as Master of the King's Musick, he was drawn back to his humble origins and frequently visited the cottage during the last years of his life.

The earliest record of Elgar's Birthplace is from 1828, although at least part of the building dates from the previous century. In May 1935 the cottage was sold 'to the Mayor, Alderman and Citizens of the City of Worcester.' Under the leadership of Elgar's daughter, Mrs Carice Elgar Blake, a group of trustees agreed to take responsibility for raising the capital to finance the creation of a museum. Immediate assistance came from a campaign organised by the editor of the Daily Telegraph which collected nearly £2,600. On 3 September 1935, during the Worcester Three Choirs Festival, the Lord Lieutenant of Worcestershire unveiled the Elgar Memorial window in the north aisle of the Cathedral. The event attracted many distinguished musicians to Worcester, a number of whom took the opportunity to travel out to Broadheath, signing the Visitors' Book before they left.

Carice Elgar Blake now lived in Broadheath, having moved there in November 1936 with her husband, Samuel. She was able to organise the work necessary to turn the cottage, until recently inhabited, into a place for visitors. In 1938 work began on the fabric, enabling the museum to open that summer in time for the Worcester Three Choirs Festival week in September.

During the first months of 1939 the first curator was appointed and moved to live in the museum in the spring. This greatly assisted Carice Elgar who had to nurse her husband during the final months of his life and, just before the outbreak of war, Samuel Blake died. The Museum remained open during the years of hostilities, but only began to assume a national importance in the 1950's as many of those who were to become biographers of Elgar began to use the archive for their research.

Carice Elgar Blake

The trustees, by then chaired by the composer Sir Arthur Bliss, recognising that the facilities at the cottage were barely adequate, turned their minds to improving the accommodation for the curator. They hoped to raise sufficient funds to purchase adjacent land on which to build new accommodation. However, they eventually agreed to convert the stable block at the side of the Birthplace which was ready for a new curator who took over in 1967.

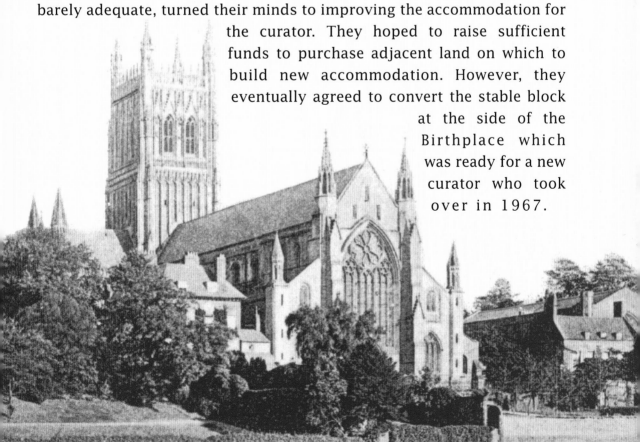

After the completion of the building work, the museum re-opened on 12 May to which many distinguished guests were invited, including the great violinist Yehudi Menuhin. His association with the trustees and the building would grow over the years, particularly when he became President of the Trust. Menuhin agreed to lead an appeal to increase funds by an additional £25,000.

In March 1968, in recognition of her thirty years of work, Carice Elgar Blake was declared President of the Trust for life. Her Presidency was, sadly, short-lived for she died in July 1970. In 1973 Wulstan Atkins, Elgar's God-son, became Chairman of the trustees. and early in his Chairmanship a new appeal for £100,000 was

Dame Janet Baker,
opening the new Centre in October 2000.

launched. During this time the Birthplace cottage was in constant need of attention, and absorbed much of the money raised. However, in 1979 the trustees were able to purchase a nearby house, Rose Cottage, which enabled the curator to move out of the Birthplace at last.

In March 1990 the trustees launched the Birthplace Development Appeal with a view to constructing a visitor centre, with improved display facilities, adjacent to the Birthplace cottage. With support from the Heritage Lottery Fund and other organisations including Worcestershire County Council and the Foundation for Sport and the Arts, the doors of the new centre were opened in August 2000 and on 19 October Dame Janet Baker, joint President of the Trust, officiated at the formal opening. The Birthplace was at last able to make its contribution to Elgarian conservation, research and education, while enabling many more people to enjoy learning about the composer and hearing his music.

Elgar's Birthplace, despite the short time he lived there, is a place redolent with the atmosphere of his life and music. Here we can discover the story of his life and learn something of his music, both of which have much to tell us today. It is to be hoped that this booklet will enable visitors to recall their time in Broadheath and the importance of preserving Elgar's memorial for future generations.

Andrew Neill

The Visitor Centre

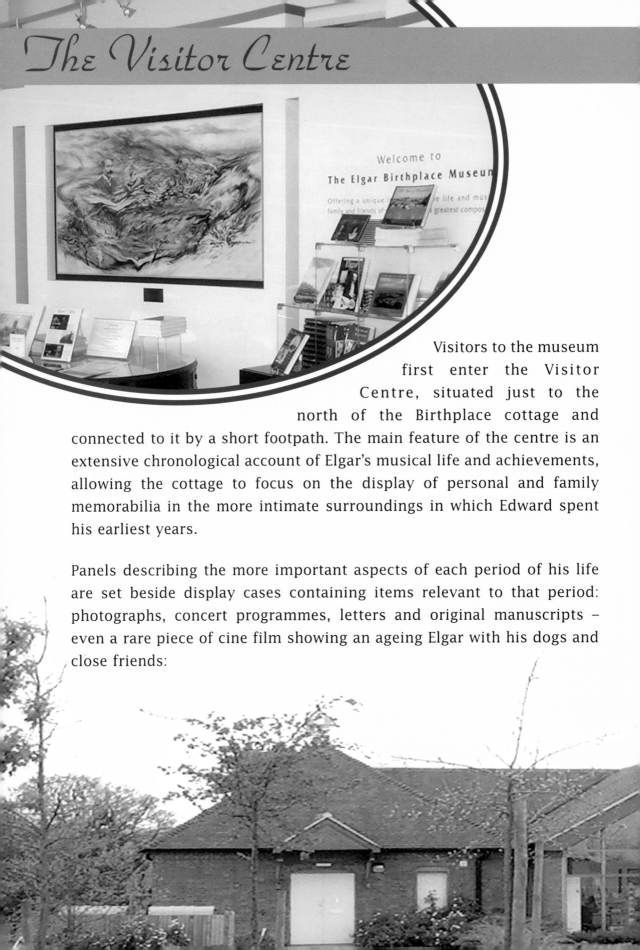

Visitors to the museum first enter the Visitor Centre, situated just to the north of the Birthplace cottage and connected to it by a short footpath. The main feature of the centre is an extensive chronological account of Elgar's musical life and achievements, allowing the cottage to focus on the display of personal and family memorabilia in the more intimate surroundings in which Edward spent his earliest years.

Panels describing the more important aspects of each period of his life are set beside display cases containing items relevant to that period: photographs, concert programmes, letters and original manuscripts – even a rare piece of cine film showing an ageing Elgar with his dogs and close friends:

Boyhood Years tells the story of early family music making;

A Time for Learning, in which we can see Elgar's early attempts at composition, and his chores as a local musician;

The Malvern Years is the time when his music really started to develop, and culminated with the composition of the Enigma Variations, Dream of Gerontius and the Pomp & Circumstance Marches;

The Hereford Years: the "high summer" of Elgar's creative output, with the two symphonies, Introduction & Allegro and the violin concerto;

London and the War saw the composition of Falstaff and several pieces for charity;

A Country Retreat tells of Elgar's time in the Sussex countryside, when he composed his chamber music and his great cello concerto;

Finale: After the death of his wife, Elgar retreats to Worcestershire.

There is a special display of Elgar's honours which includes his magnificent doctoral robes ...

... and his many medals.

Other displays tell the story of the composition of the Enigma Variations, his recording career, his musical collaborations with his wife, and his versatility as a composer – all with handsets to give musical examples.

And one display case is reserved for a regularly changing exhibition on a specific, usually topical aspect of the composer's life.

The centre's multi-purpose Carice Elgar Room is used throughout the year for meetings, occasional chamber concerts, exhibitions, craft fairs and other special events. When it is not being used for these purposes, visitors can sit and enjoy a cup of coffee before moving on to the cottage or browsing in the museum shop.

The shop almost certainly offers the world's greatest selection of recordings of Elgar's music, whether the latest release from a top rank orchestra or a historical recording conducted by Elgar himself, carefully reprocessed and transferred to CD. Visitors have the opportunity to listen to a selection of recordings if they wish before making their purchase, and there is always Elgar's 'music all around'. The shop also stocks a wide range of books about Elgar, scores of his music, greetings cards, souvenirs and gifts, mainly with a musical theme. Many have been made exclusively for the Birthplace, making them attractive and unusual presents.

The Study

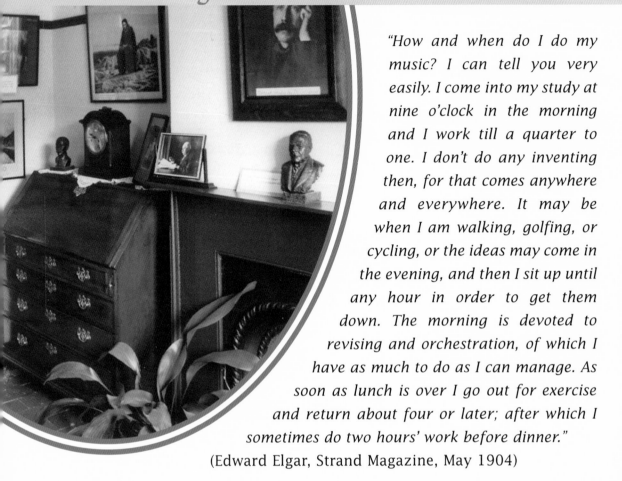

"How and when do I do my music? I can tell you very easily. I come into my study at nine o'clock in the morning and I work till a quarter to one. I don't do any inventing then, for that comes anywhere and everywhere. It may be when I am walking, golfing, or cycling, or the ideas may come in the evening, and then I sit up until any hour in order to get them down. The morning is devoted to revising and orchestration, of which I have as much to do as I can manage. As soon as lunch is over I go out for exercise and return about four or later; after which I sometimes do two hours' work before dinner."

(Edward Elgar, Strand Magazine, May 1904)

On the ground floor of the Birthplace cottage, Elgar's "Study" was originally set up by his daughter, Carice Elgar Blake. It captures the atmosphere of her father's study and contains objects that he would have used daily throughout his composing life. The room is dominated by the large leather-topped desk crowded with writing utensils. Elgar bought this desk in a second-hand shop in London in 1889, the same year that he married Caroline Alice Roberts. It was to go with them to all their later homes.

Seated before it in his "bosun's chair", Elgar had by him all the things that are now on display. The quotation from Mozart, copied in Elgar's own hand, was always placed in view, offering a constant source of inspiration:

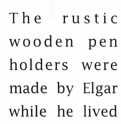

"the passions, whether violent or otherwise, must never be expressed to disgust, – and music, even in the most terrific situation, never give pain to the ear; but ever delight it and remain Music"

(W.A. Mozart, Wien 1781)

The rustic wooden pen holders were made by Elgar while he lived at Brinkwells, near Fittleworth, in the Sussex woods. Elgar's pens are also on display, along with the rubber stamps with which he would annotate his musical sketches and scores. His manuscript paper was often painstakingly prepared by his wife, Alice, complete with bar lines and instrument names. Resting on top are the five-pronged stave pens she used.

Elgar's own glass-fronted bookcase contains a selection of books from his extensive library, carefully chosen by Carice as important sources of inspiration and reference for many of his major compositions.

This room also contains one of Elgar's many gramophones. His interest in recording technology grew as the industry developed and in the last twenty years of his life he produced a remarkable series of composer-conducted recordings embracing most of his major orchestral works.

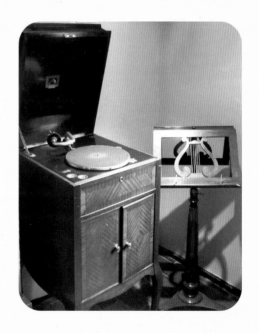

The walls are hung with a variety of portrait photographs from all periods of Elgar's adult life. Seen together, these make a memorable impression of the man himself.

"How well I remember the day he was born. The air was sweet with the perfume of flowers, bees were humming and all the earth was lovely. There seemed to be, to we little ones, a lot of unnecessary running about in the house, and Father came tearing up the drive with a strange man in the carriage ... we were taken a scamper across the heath to be out of the way."

(Elgar's sister Lucy, reminiscing in 1912)

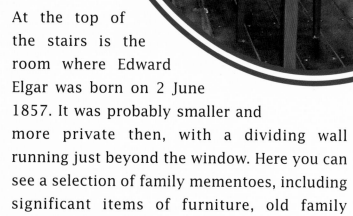
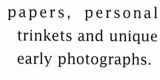

At the top of the stairs is the room where Edward Elgar was born on 2 June 1857. It was probably smaller and more private then, with a dividing wall running just beyond the window. Here you can see a selection of family mementoes, including significant items of furniture, old family papers, personal trinkets and unique early photographs.

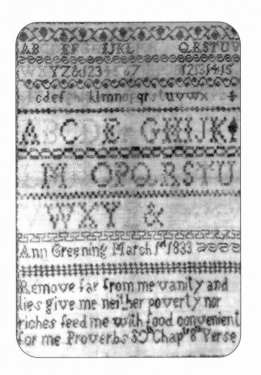

There is a selection of samplers and patchworks made by Elgar's mother and grandmother. There is also a mock concert programme by Elgar's Uncle Thomas that demonstrates the same quirky Elgarian sense of humour seen in Elgar's own letters and sketches, as well as a collection of advertisements, business cards and concert and performance tickets belonging to Elgar and his father. A display cabinet

houses items belonging to his parents, his brothers and sisters, and his wife and daughter. Of particular interest are the birth and marriage certificates, and the tiny toys that belonged to his younger brother Joe (the 'Beethoven' of the family) who sadly died when only seven years old.

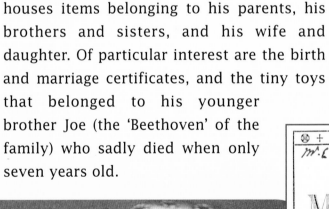

There are items relating to Elgar's marriage to Caroline Alice Roberts on 8 May 1889. These include a Grainger & Co cider-set which was presented to them on their wedding day, and the carved Indian animals that Alice brought with her as a memory of her childhood in India.

There can also be seen a fascinating and unique collection of Elgar's humorous pencil sketches.

Finally, above the stairs there is the last public portrait of Elgar, taken at the Three Choirs Festival in Hereford, 1933. It eloquently demonstrates the fulfilment of his early musical ambition fostered here in his place of birth.

The Hobbies Room

It has been said that Elgar liked to give the impression of a country gentleman who, after a round of golf, would come home and just happen to write some of England's greatest music. While these accounts should not be taken too literally, it is true that Elgar often had to be bullied into work, and when the creative juices were not flowing there was a vast array of hobbies to be pursued. This room illustrates some of them, revealing a fascinating picture of the man behind the musician. They include:

- **outdoor pursuits**, such as cycling, walking the Malvern Hills, flying home-made kites, fishing in the River Teme and cultivating roses in his garden. In the room can be found examples of his woodworking, including pen holders and pokerwork. And Elgar's cycling maps, marked with the routes he followed along the lanes of Worcestershire and Herefordshire, are evidence of the extent of his excursions.

- **science and technology**: at Plas Gwyn, his home in Hereford from 1904 until 1911, he converted an outhouse into a laboratory which he called 'The Ark'. Here he conducted experiments, made soap and even invented a piece of equipment for making sulphuretted hydrogen. This is displayed, along with one of Elgar's microscopes, a set of slides and related books.

- **animals**: as a bachelor, Elgar kept dogs but his wife Alice was not a "doggy person". After her death, dogs including Meg, Marco and Mina once more became his constant companions. On the evening of his 70th birthday, at the end of a prestigious concert broadcast live on BBC radio, he stepped up to the microphone and said: "Good night everybody. Good night, Marco." Horses were also important to Elgar and, in the 1920s, he developed a serious interest in horse racing, becoming a member of Worcester Race Club. His badge and membership card are on display.

- **literature**, a passion inherited from his mother. Wherever he went, Elgar spent many hours browsing in second-hand book shops. He built up a large library, some examples of which can be seen in the bookcase to the right of the fireplace. Edward's mother, Ann Elgar, was a devotee of the poet Longfellow, and Elgar inherited her tastes, basing several of his musical compositions on the poet's works – indeed, Elgar became so familiar with *Hyperion* that he noted in the margin of his copy any differences from earlier editions.

- **puzzles and puns**: Some examples of the ciphers he devised can be found in the drawers beneath the science cabinet. Elgar and Alice had their own intimate language, a sort of baby talk. Thus, in 1912 Alice wrote at the foot of a poem to Elgar *"For my Beloved's booful music. Pease not beat. Will dis do?"*, to which he responded *"Vessy nice"*.

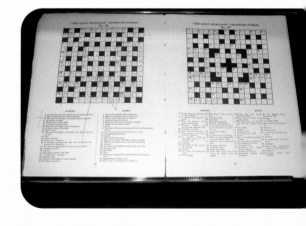

He and his daughter, Carice, were crossword puzzle enthusiasts, often competing playfully against each other. Examples of crosswords completed in Elgar's hand are displayed; that in the framed copy of the *Daily Telegraph* is surrounded by doodles, not unlike his letters and postcards and the margins of his books, which are often filled with witty comments and embellished with funny sketches and cartoons.

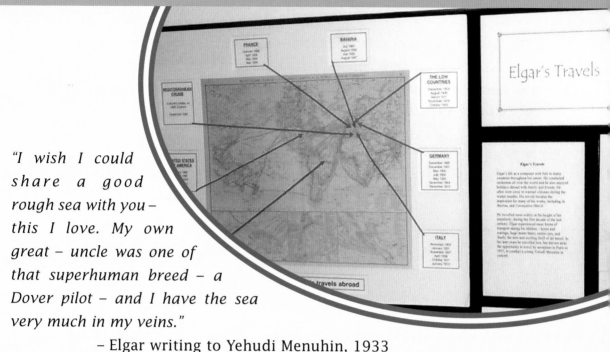

Elgar's Travels

Elgar's Travels

travels abroad

"I wish I could share a good rough sea with you – this I love. My own great – uncle was one of that superhuman breed – a Dover pilot – and I have the sea very much in my veins."

– Elgar writing to Yehudi Menuhin, 1933

This room explores a theme that recurs throughout Elgar's life: the need for change and the new creative stimulation it could bring. This is revealed in Elgar's frequent changes of home, his explorations of the countryside and his travels both in this country and abroad. Many of his greatest works found their inspiration through his experience of new sights and sounds.

Elgar was introduced to travel at an early age by his father whom he accompanied around Worcestershire in the family pony and trap. Throughout his life he continued to travel, and was fortunate to live during a period of rapid development in transportation. He was to experience the joys of travelling by bicycle, steam-train, packet steamer, motor car, ocean liner and even aeroplane. Displayed here are a selection of fascinating items saved from Elgar's holidays abroad.

SPECIAL CRUISES

1,000 MILES of the AMAZON
IN AN OCEAN LINER

THE BOOTH
STEAMSHIP COMPANY Ltd.

There are also passports, a cast of his hand taken in Rome 1907, and a brochure from his 1923 holiday *1000 Miles up the Amazon* with The Booth Steamship Company Ltd.

Of especial note is the description of Elgar in his 1919 passport – height 5ft 10in, with "ordinary mouth and chin", "large aquiline" nose, "fair" complexion, "oval" face and "white-grey" hair. Elgar's holidays abroad often lasted for several weeks or months. They were not purely for relaxation, but combined sightseeing, concert-going, conducting engagements and work such as orchestrating and correcting proofs.

Many of his holidays involved intricate organisation including the need to pack for all types of social occasion. The journey was often time-consuming, dirty, and exhausting, and the holiday itself a considerable drain on the family's already strained finances. It also meant

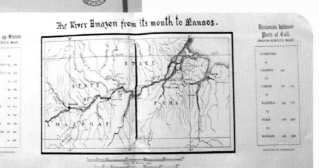

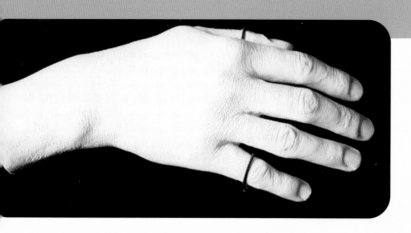

long periods away from his daughter Carice and the countryside he loved.

Nevertheless, Elgar made over thirty separate journeys abroad, sending Carice postcards telling her of his current where-abouts and what he had been up to.

Also in this room there is a display of some of the other houses in which Elgar lived – Plas Gwyn, Birchwood Lodge, Marl Bank, and Naple-ton Grange, which has been captured in a delightful water-colour by his niece, Clare Grafton.

This modest cottage in which Elgar was born is testimony to his humble beginnings, and for the most part the items displayed here reflect his personality, his interests, his activities, his friends and relationships, and his continuing contacts with the City of Worcester. He greatly esteemed the Freedom of the City that was bestowed on him in 1905 and was marked by the presentation of a handsome silver casket. Elgar's infirm father watched the procession from an upper window of the Elgar Brothers music shop on the High Street and, as the procession passed by, Elgar raised his cap in tribute to him.

One of his local friends was Sir Ivor Atkins, Organist and Master of Choristers, and the Atkins Room, the inner or second room in the cottage, is named after the Atkins family, partly to reflect that friendship but also to mark the donation of several manuscripts and scores by Sir Ivor's son Wulstan who was President of the Elgar Foundation for many years and worked for the expansion of the Museum. Rare items from the archive are displayed within the Atkins Room.

The archive, which has been built up over many years through donation and purchase and which continues to grow, is the largest single collection of material anywhere devoted to the life and music of Sir Edward Elgar. It contains over 200 original manuscripts and sketches (including the 2nd Symphony, one of the Pomp and Circumstance marches, and The Wand of Youth suites), proof scores, over 10,000 letters, family scrapbooks, press cuttings, photographs, programmes and a small working library of books and CDs.

It is housed within a small but well-equipped research centre, which is widely used by scholars and students carrying out research and is normally available, by prior arrangement, on weekdays. Because space within the centre is limited, it is essential to make an appointment. Those wishing to use the facility are invited to contact the Archivist here at the Museum.

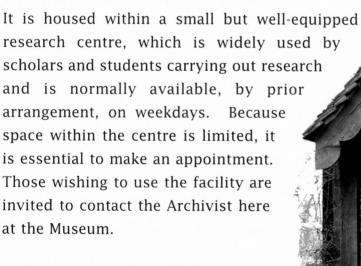

Visitors are encouraged to spend time in the garden and, thanks to well-wishers, there are plenty of benches on which to relax – some donated in memory of friends. After opening the Birthplace to the public in the 1930s, Carice had the garden re-designed, using Buckler's painting of the cottage as her inspiration. The standard roses and rose arch are still here, as are the two central paths, one of which Elgar's father kept rolled for the Elgar girls to bowl their hoops down. However in the 1850s there was also a sizeable vegetable patch, and a few chickens running around.

After a glorious display of spring bulbs, the garden really comes into its own in late spring, as the many old-fashioned cottage favourites start to appear and merge into each other. Many are left to seed themselves to give a real cottage garden effect and a riot of colour throughout the summer.

The approach of autumn brings a lovely display of Michaelmas daisies.

At the end of the path is Elgar's summer-house. This was originally in the garden of his last home, Marl Bank, and was moved here in the 1980s. Beyond the ancient yew tree, which Elgar himself would have remembered, the hedge drops away and there is a revelation – a glorious uninterrupted view of the Malvern Hills.

At the side of the path leading back to the Centre, a little headstone marks the graves of two of Elgar's dogs, Marco and Mina, his "beloved companions".

A Brief Chronology

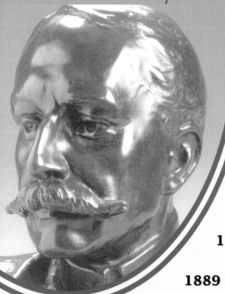

1857 Born 2 June at Broadheath
1863 Moves to 10 High Street, Worcester
1864 Starts learning the piano
1872 First complete compositions –
The Language of Flowers and *Chantant*
1877 First series of violin lessons
with Adolphe Pollitzer
1878 Plays in Three Choirs Festival Orchestra
1884 First London performance of one of his
compositions – *Sevillana*
1885 Succeeds his father as organist of St George's RC
Church, Worcester
1889 Marries Caroline Alice Roberts at Brompton
Oratory, South Kensington; moves to London
1890 Daughter Carice born 14 August
1891 Returns to Worcestershire; moves to Forli, Malvern Link
1897 Worcestershire Philharmonic Society formed with Elgar as conductor
1899 Moves to Craeg Lea, Malvern Wells
1900 Awarded Doctorate by Cambridge University
1904 Three day Elgar Festival at Covent Garden;
Knighted; moves to Plas Gwyn, Hereford
Accepts post of Peyton Professor of Music at Birmingham University
1905 First visit to USA; honorary doctorate from Yale University
1911 Becomes member of the Order of Merit
Succeeds Richter as conductor of London Symphony Orchestra
1912 Moves to Severn House, Hampstead, London
1914 Conducts his first gramophone recording – *Carissima*
1920 Wife Alice dies 7 April
1923 Returns to Worcestershire; visits South America for cruise up
Amazon
1924 Appointed Master of the King's Musick
1925 Awarded Gold medal of the Royal Philharmonic Society
1928 Awarded KCVO
1931 Opens EMI studios at Abbey Road, London
1932 Conducts Yehudi Menuhin in recording of the Violin Concerto
1933 Flies to Paris to conduct performance of the Violin Concerto;
visits Delius at Grez-sur-Loing; Awarded GCVO
1934 Dies peacefully on 23 February in Worcester
1935 Birthplace Cottage purchased by Worcester City Council

1888 Salut d'Amour

1890 Froissart

1892 Serenade for Strings

1893 The Black Knight

1894 The Snow; Fly, Singing Bird

1895 Organ Sonata No.1

1896 From the Bavarian Highlands;
The Light of Life (Lux Christi); King Olaf

1897 Imperial March; The Banner of St George;
Chanson de Nuit

1898 Caractacus

1899 Sea Pictures; Chanson de Matin;
Variations on an Original Theme (Enigma Variations)

1900 The Dream of Gerontius

1901 Pomp and Circumstance Marches Nos.1 and 2;
Cockaigne (In London Town)

1902 Coronation Ode

1903 The Apostles

1904 Pomp and Circumstance March No.3; In the South (Alassio)

1905 Introduction and Allegro for Strings

1906 The Kingdom

1907 Pomp and Circumstance March No.4; Wand of Youth Suite No.1

1908 Symphony No.1; Wand of Youth Suite No.2

1910 Violin Concerto

1911 Symphony No.2; Coronation March

1912 Crown of India; Great is the Lord (Psalm 48); The Music Makers

1913 Falstaff

1914 Sospiri; Give unto the Lord (Psalm 29)

1915 Polonia; The Starlight Express; Une Voix dans le Désert

1916 Le Drapeau Belge; The Spirit of England

1917 The Fringes of the Fleet; The Sanguine Fan

1918 Violin Sonata; String Quartet

1919 Piano Quintet; Cello Concerto

1924 Empire March

1930 Severn Suite for brass band; Pomp and Circumstance March No.5

1931 Nursery Suite

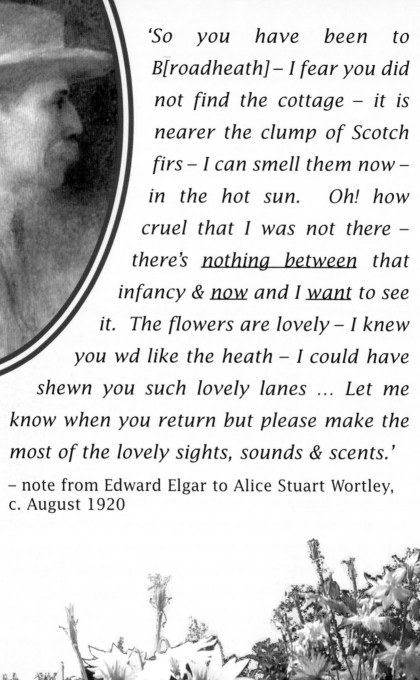

'So you have been to B[roadheath] – I fear you did not find the cottage – it is nearer the clump of Scotch firs – I can smell them now – in the hot sun. Oh! how cruel that I was not there – there's <u>nothing between</u> that infancy & <u>now</u> and I <u>want</u> to see it. The flowers are lovely – I knew you wd like the heath – I could have shewn you such lovely lanes … Let me know when you return but please make the most of the lovely sights, sounds & scents.'

– note from Edward Elgar to Alice Stuart Wortley,
c. August 1920